KAHLIL

GIBRAN

Boundless Sorrow

&

Unclouded Joy

(Selected Quotes & Poems)

Murat Durmus
(editor & contributor)

i

Murat Durmus (editor & contributor)

978-1-4716-6595-0

Imprint: Lulu.com (self-published)

About the Author

Murat Durmus is CEO and founder of AISOMA (a Frankfurt am Main (Germany) based company specialized in AI-based technology development and consulting) and Author of the books THEAI THOUGHT BOOK & INSIDE ALAN TURING.

You can get in touch with the Author via LinkedIn:

E-Mail: murat.durmus@aisoma.de

*"You talk when you cease
to be at peace with your thoughts."*

~ Kahlil Gibran

Contents

FOREWORD

For most, the name Gibran brings to mind his famous work "The Prophet," which first appeared in New York in 1923 and quickly became a worldwide cult book. The editions in many languages indicate how extensive and existentially intense this poet's work is.

He also left lasting impressions as a painter. He has become an essential bridge-builder between religions through his life between the Levant, Europe, and America, his poetry, his many aphorisms, and his unique stories.

I hope this little booklet with a selection of some of his most beautiful and inspiring quotes and poems will touch you as much as it has touched me.

"God judges a tree by its fruits and not by its roots."

~ Paulo Coelho

Murat Durmus
14 June 2022

INTRODUCTION

Kahlil Gibran was born in January 1883 in Bisharri, Lebanon. In 1895 he emigrated with his mother, sisters, and half-brother to Boston in the USA.

Kamila Gibran, his mother, was the daughter of the priest Istiphan Rahmeh. The misspelling of Kahlil Gibran is due to the anglicization of his name in the Boston elementary school he attended.

In his youth, Gibran was a protégé of photographer and publicist F. Holland Day. After returning to Lebanon, Gibran studied art, French, Arabic, and Arabic literature in 1897.

In 1899, he returned to Boston via Paris. In 1903 his mother, his half-brother Butrus (* 1877), and his younger sister Sultanah (* 1887) died of tuberculosis. In 1904 he had his first success as a painter.

From 1908 he studied art and European literature in Paris. In 1912 he moved to New York.

The autobiographical novel Broken Wings appeared in the same year. Finally, in 1918, The Madman appeared, the first book he had written in English.

He was the founding president of the literary association Arrabitah and belonged to the Maronite Christian Church.

He died of liver cancer in New York on April 10, 1931, and was buried in his birthplace in Lebanon.

Work and thought

The central motifs of his poetry and philosophical thought revolve around the idea that life, love, and death should be the essentials for us humans.

His work is seen as a link between the philosophical directions of the Orient, e.g., Sufism, and the Western philosophies influenced by Christianity.

The Prophet, published in 1923, is considered his best known as Gibran's preparatory work. Like many of his other writings, it was illustrated by himself.

Gibran wrote most of his early works in Arabic, but from 1918 onward, he wrote mainly in English; His poetic and linguistically panoramic images are particularly captivating.

In his spiritual aphorisms and worldly wisdom, he was always concerned with touching the heart of his listeners.

KAHLIL GIBRAN

(January 6, 1883 – April 10, 1931)

You talk when you cease to be at peace with your thoughts.

(The Prophet)

Out of suffering have emerged the strongest souls; the most massive characters are seared with scars.

If you love somebody, let them go, for if they return, they were always yours. If they don't, they never were.

Trees are poems the earth writes upon the sky,

We fell them down and turn them into paper,

That we may record our emptiness.

Ever has it been that love knows not its own depth until the hour of separation.

When you are sorrowful look again in your heart, and you shall see that in truth you are weeping for that which has been your delight.

Beauty is not in the face; beauty is a light in the heart.

I have found both freedom and safety in my madness; the freedom of loneliness and the safety from being understood, for those who understand us enslave something in us.

(The Madman)

I have learned silence from the talkative, toleration from the intolerant, and kindness from the unkind; yet strange, I am ungrateful to these teachers.

Tenderness and kindness are not signs of weakness and despair, but manifestations of strength and resolution.

Some of you say, "Joy is greater than sorrow," and others say, "Nay, sorrow is the greater."

But I say unto you, they are inseparable.

Together they come, and when one sits alone with you at your board, remember that the other is asleep upon your bed.

(The Prophet)

You give but little when you give of your possessions.

It is when you give of yourself that you truly give.

(The Prophet)

It takes a minute to have a crush on someone, an hour to like someone, and a day to love someone ...

but it takes a lifetime to forget someone

No human relation gives one possession in another — every two souls are absolutely different.

In friendship or in love, the two side by side raise hands together to find what one cannot reach alone.

For what is it to die but to stand naked in the wind and to melt into the sun?

And when the earth shall claim your limbs, then shall you truly dance.

Beauty is eternity gazing at itself in a mirror.

But you are eternity and you are the mirror.

We choose our joys and sorrows long before we experience them.

The smallest act of kindness is worth more than the greatest intention.

(The Essential Kahlil Gibran)

The Reality of The Other Person Lies Not In What He Reveals To You, But What He Cannot Reveal To You.

Therefore, If You Would Understand Him, Listen Not To What He Says, But Rather To What He Does Not Say.

You may forget with whom you laughed, but you will never forget with whom you wept.

(Sand and Foam)

Music is the language of the spirit. It opens the secret of life bringing peace, abolishing strife.

Solitude has soft, silky hands, but with strong fingers it
grasps the heart and makes it ache with sorrow.

(The Broken Wings)

To understand the heart and mind of a person,

look not at what he has already achieved,

but at what he aspires to.

(The Madman)

The appearance of things changes according to the emotions;
and thus, we see magic and beauty in them, while the magic
and beauty are really in ourselves.

(The Broken Wings)

We wanderers, ever seeking the lonelier way, begin no day
where we have ended another day; and no sunrise finds us
where sunset left us. Even while the earth sleeps, we travel.
We are the seeds of the tenacious plant, and it is in our ripeness

and our fullness of heart that we are given to the wind and are scattered.

(The Prophet)

You have been told that, even like a chain, you are as weak as your weakest link.

This is but half the truth.

You are also as strong as your strongest link.

To measure you by your smallest deed is to reckon the power of the ocean

by the frailty of its foam.

To judge you by your failures is to cast blame upon the seasons for their inconstancy.

(The Prophet)

If you reveal your secrets to the wind,

you should not blame the wind for

revealing them to the trees.

(The Wanderer)

Your living is determined not so much by what life brings to you as by the attitude you bring to life; not so much by what happens to you as by the way your mind looks at what happens.

Keep me away from the wisdom which does not cry, the philosophy which does not laugh and the greatness which does not bow before children.

(Mirror of the Soul)

Thus, with my lips have I denounced you, while my heart, bleeding within me, called you tender names.

It was love lashed by its own self that spoke. It was pride half slain that fluttered in the dust. It was my hunger for your love that raged from the housetop, while my own love, kneeling in silence, prayed your forgiveness.

(The Forerunner: His Parables and Poems)

Trust in dreams, for in them is the hidden gate to eternity.

One's own religion is after all a matter between oneself and one's Maker and no one else's.

Say not, "I have found the truth," but rather, "I have found a truth."

Say not, "I have found the path of the soul." Say rather, "I have met the soul walking upon my path."

For the soul walks upon all paths.

The soul walks not upon a line, neither does it grow like a reed.

The soul unfolds itself, like a lotus of countless petals.

(The Prophet)

An eye for an eye, and the whole world would be blind.

The optimist sees the rose and not its thorns; the pessimist stares at the thorns, oblivious to the rose.

Travel and tell no one, live a true love story and tell no one, live happily and tell no one, people ruin beautiful things.

Sadness is but a wall between two gardens.

(Sand and Foam)

Forgetfulness is a form of freedom.

For what is evil but good tortured by its own hunger and thirst?

(The Prophet)

Only yesterday I was no different than them, yet I was saved. I am explaining to you the way of life of a people who say every sort of wicked thing about me because I sacrificed their friendship to gain my own soul. I left the dark paths of their duplicity and turned my eyes toward the light where there is salvation, truth, and justice. They have exiled me now from their society, yet I am content. Mankind only exiles the one whose large spirit rebels against injustice and tyranny. He who does not prefer exile to servility is not free in the true and necessary sense of freedom.

A friend who is far away is sometimes much nearer than one who is at hand. Is not the mountain far more awe-inspiring and more clearly visible to one passing through the valley than to those who inhabit the mountain?

Pity the nation that is full of beliefs and empty of religion.

Pity the nation that wears a cloth it does not weave

and eats a bread it does not harvest.

Pity the nation that acclaims the bully as hero,

and that deems the glittering conqueror bountiful.

Pity a nation that despises a passion in its dream,

yet submits in its awakening.

Pity the nation that raises not its voice

save when it walks in a funeral,

boasts not except among its ruins,

and will rebel not save when its neck is laid

between the sword and the block.

Pity the nation whose statesman is a fox,

whose philosopher is a juggler,

and whose art is the art of patching and mimicking

Pity the nation that welcomes its new ruler with trumpeting,

and farewells him with hooting,

only to welcome another with trumpeting again.

Pity the nation whose sages are dumb with years

and whose strongmen are yet in the cradle.

Pity the nation divided into fragments,

each fragment deeming itself a nation.

(The Garden of The Prophet)

In one drop of water are found all the secrets of all the
oceans;

in one aspect of You are found all the aspects of existence.

And God said "Love Your Enemy," and I obeyed him and
loved myself.

(The Broken Wings)

Many of us spend our whole lives running from feeling with
the mistaken belief that you cannot bear the pain. But you
have already borne the pain. What you have not done is feel
all you are beyond that pain.

Faith is an oasis in the heart which will never be reached by
the caravan of thinking.

Seven times I have despised my soul:

The first time when I saw her being meek that she might attain height.

The second time when I saw her limping before the crippled.

The third time when she was given to choose between the hard and the easy, and she chose the easy.

The fourth time when she committed a wrong, and comforted herself that others also commit wrong.

The fifth time when she forbode for weakness, and attributed her patience to strength.

The sixth time when she despised the ugliness of a face, and knew not that it was one of her own masks.

And the seventh time when she sang a song of praise, and deemed it a virtue.

(Sand and Foam)

The teacher who is indeed wise does not bid you to enter the house of his wisdom but rather leads you to the threshold of your mind.

I wash my hands of those who imagine chattering to be knowledge,

silence to be ignorance, and affection to be art.

When life does not find a singer to sing her heart, she produces a philosopher to speak her mind.

(Sand and Foam)

Your reason and your passion are the rudder and the sails of your seafaring soul.

If either your sails or your rudder be broken, you can but toss and drift, or else be held at a standstill in mid-seas.

For reason, ruling alone, is a force confining; and passion, unattended, is a flame that burns to its own destruction.

Therefore, let your soul exalt your reason to the height of passion, that it may sing;

And let it direct your passion with reason, that your passion may live through its own daily resurrection, and like the phoenix rise above its own ashes.

Desire is half of life; indifference is half of death.

(Sand and Foam)

Yesterday we obeyed kings and bent our necks before emperors. But today we kneel only to truth, follow only beauty, and obey only love.

(The Vision: Reflections on the Way of the Soul)

Life without liberty is like a body without spirit.

(The Vision: Reflections on the Way of the Soul)

The most pitiful among men is he who turns his dreams into silver and gold.

Of the good in you I can speak, but not of the evil.

For what is evil but good tortured by its own hunger and thirst?

Verily when good is hungry it seeks food even in dark caves, and when it thirsts it drinks even of dead waters.

(The Prophet)

When you are joyous, look deep into your heart and you shall find it is only that which has given you sorrow that is giving you joy. When you are sorrowful look again in your heart, and you shall see that in truth you are weeping for that which has been your delight.

Do not fear the thorns in your path, for they draw only corrupt blood.

Modern civilization has made woman a little wiser, but it has increased her suffering because of man's covetousness. The woman of yesterday was a happy wife, but the woman of today is a miserable mistress. In the past she walked blindly in the light, but now she walks open-eyed in the dark. She was beautiful in her ignorance, virtuous in her simplicity, and strong in her weakness. Today she has become ugly in her ingenuity, superficial and heartless in her knowledge. Will the day ever come when beauty and knowledge, ingenuity and virtue, and weakness of body and strength of spirit will be united in a woman?

(Broken Wings)

Strange, the desire for certain pleasures is a part of my pain.

(Sand and Foam)

Oftentimes we call Life bitter names, but only when we ourselves are bitter and dark. And we deem her empty and unprofitable, but only when the soul goes wandering in desolate places, and the heart is drunken with overmindfulness of self.

Life is deep and high and distant; and though only your vast vision can reach even her feet, yet she is near; and though only the breath of your breath reaches her heart, the shadow of your shadow crosses her face, and the echo of your faintest cry becomes a spring and an autumn in her breast.

And life is veiled and hidden, even as your greater self is hidden and veiled. Yet when Life speaks, all the winds become words; and when she speaks again, the smiles upon your lips and the tears in your eyes turn also into words. When she sings, the deaf hear and are held; and when she comes walking, the sightless behold her and are amazed and follow her in wonder and astonishment.

(The Garden of The Prophet)

Our anxiety does not come from thinking about the future,
but from wanting to control it.

To measure you by your smallest deed

is to reckon the ocean by the frailty of its foam.

To judge you by your failures

is to cast blame upon the seasons

for their inconsistencies.

Observe the wonders as they occur around you.

Don't claim them. Feel the artistry moving through and be
silent.

Love is the only freedom in the world because it so elevates
the spirit that the laws of humanity and the phenomena of
nature do not alter its course.

(Broken Wings)

Your pain is the breaking of the shell that encloses your understanding.

Generosity is not in giving me that which I need more than you do, but it is in giving me that which you need more than I do.

(Sand and Foam)

For thought is a bird of space, that in a cage of words may indeed unfold its wings but cannot fly.

Your reason and your passion are your rudder and sails of your seafaring soul, if either your sails or your rudder be broken, you can but toss and drift, or else be held at a standstill in mid-seas. For reason, ruling alone, is a force confining; and passion, unattended, is a flame that burns to its own destruction.

I would not exchange the laughter of my heart for the fortunes of the multitudes.

A friend who is far away is sometimes much nearer than one who is at hand.

I am the lover's gift; I am the wedding wreath;

I am the memory of a moment of happiness;

I am the last gift of the living to the dead;

I am a part of joy and a part of sorrow.

When you were a wandering desire in the mist, I too was there, a wandering desire. Then we sought one another, and out of our eagerness dreams were born. And dreams were time limitless, and dreams were space without measure.

(Sand and Foam / The Forerunner)

Love provided me with a tongue and tears.

(Broken Wings)

Let there be spaces in your togetherness.

Life is an island in an ocean of solitude and seclusion.

Life is an island, rocks are its desires, trees its dreams, and flowers its loneliness, and it is in the middle of an ocean of solitude and seclusion.

Your life, my friend, is an island separated from all other islands and continents. Regardless of how many boats you send to other shores, you yourself are an island separated by its own pains,secluded its happiness and far away in its compassion and hidden in its secrets and mysteries.

I saw you, my friend, sitting upon a mound of gold, happy in your wealth and great in your riches and believing that a handful of gold is the secret chain that links the thoughts of the people with your own thoughts and links their feeling with your own.

I saw you as a great conqueror leading a conquering army toward the fortress, then destroying and capturing it.

On second glance I found beyond the wall of your treasures a heart trembling in its solitude and seclusion like the trembling of a thirsty man within a cage of gold and jewels, but without water.

I saw you, my friend, sitting on a throne of glory surrounded by people extolling your charity, enumerating your gifts, gazing upon you as if they were in the presence of a prophet lifting their souls up into the planets and stars. I saw you looking at them, contentment and strength upon your face, as if you were to them as the soul is to the body.

On the second look I saw your secluded self standing beside your throne, suffering in its seclusion and quaking in its loneliness. I saw that self stretching its hands as if begging from unseen ghosts. I saw it looking above the shoulders of the people to a far horizon, empty of everything except its solitude and seclusion.

I saw you, my friend, passionately in love with a beautiful woman, filling her palms with your kisses as she looked at you with sympathy and affection in her eyes and sweetness of motherhood on her lips; I said, secretly, that love has erased his solitude and removed his seclusion and he is now within the eternal soul which draws toward itself, with love, those who were separated by solitude and seclusion.

On the second look I saw behind your soul another lonely soul, like a fog, trying in vain to become a drop of tears in the palm of that woman.

Your life, my friend, is a residence far away from any other residence and neighbors.

Your inner soul is a home far away from other homes named after you. If this residence is dark, you cannot light it with your neighbor's lamp; if it is empty, you cannot fill it with the riches of your neighbor; were it in the middle of a desert, you could not move it to a garden planted by someone else.

Your inner soul, my friend, is surrounded with solitude and seclusion. Were it not for this solitude and this seclusion you would not be you and I would not be I.

If it were not for that solitude and seclusion, I would, if I heard your voice, think myself to be speaking; yet, if I saw your face, I would imagine that I were looking into a mirror.

(Mirrors of the Soul)

Beauty is life when life unveils her holy face. But you are life and you are the veil. Beauty is eternity gazing at itself in a mirror. But you are eternity and you are the mirror.

(The Prophet)

But if in your fear you would seek only love's peace and love's pleasure, then it is better for you that you cover your nakedness and pass out of love's threshing-floor, into the seasonless world where you shall laugh, but not all of your laughter, and weep, but not all of your tears.

(The Prophet)

Faith is a knowledge within the heart, beyond the reach of proof

Doubt is a pain too lonely to know that faith is his twin brother.

You may chain my hands, you may shackle my feet; you may even throw me into a dark prison; but you shall not enslave my thinking, because it is free!

When you work you fulfill a part of earth's furthest dream, assigned to you when that dream was born,

And what is it to work with love?

It is to weave the cloth with threads drawn from your heart, even as if your beloved were to wear that cloth.

It is to build a house with affection, even as if your beloved were to dwell in that house.

It is to sow seeds with tenderness and reap the harvest with joy, even as if your beloved were to eat the fruit.

It is to charge all things you fashion with a breath of your own spirit.

Work is love made visible.

(The Prophet)

The philosopher's soul dwells in his head, the poet's soul is in his heart; the singer's soul lingers about his throat, but the soul of the dancer abides in all her body.

Where are you now, my beloved?

Do you hear my weeping from beyond the ocean?

Do you understand my need?

Do you know the greatness of my patience?

(Love Letters in the Sand: The Love Poems of Khalil Gibran)

POEMS

ON CHILDREN

And a woman who held a babe against her bosom said,
Speak to us of Children.

And he said:

Your children are not your children.

They are the sons and daughters of Life's longing for itself.

They come through you but not from you,

And though they are with you yet they belong not to you.

You may give them your love but not your thoughts,

For they have their own thoughts.

You may house their bodies but not their souls,

For their souls dwell in the house of tomorrow, which you
cannot visit, not even in your dreams.

You may strive to be like them, but seek not to make them
like you.

For life goes not backward nor tarries with yesterday.

You are the bows from which your children as living arrows
are sent forth.

The archer sees the mark upon the path of the infinite, and He bends you with His might that His arrows may go swift and far.

Let your bending in the archer's hand be for gladness;

For even as He loves the arrow that flies, so He loves also the bow that is stable.

The Prophet (Knopf, 1923).

ON LOVE

Then said Almitra, Speak to us of Love.

And he raised his head and looked upon the people, and there fell a stillness upon them. And with a great voice he said:

When love beckons to you, follow him,

Though his ways are hard and steep.

And when his wings enfold you yield to him,

Though the sword hidden among his pinions may wound you.

And when he speaks to you believe in him,

Though his voice may shatter your dreams as the north wind lays waste the garden.

For even as love crowns you so shall he crucify you. Even as he is for your growth so is he for your pruning.

Even as he ascends to your height and caresses your tenderest branches that quiver in the sun,

So shall he descend to your roots and shake them in their clinging to the earth.

Like sheaves of corn he gathers you unto himself

He threshes you to make your naked.

He sifts you to free you from your husks.

He grinds you to whiteness.

He kneads you until you are pliant;

And then he assigns you to his sacred fire, that you may become sacred bread for God's sacred feast.

All these things shall love do unto you that you may know the secrets of your heart, and in that knowledge become a fragment of Life's heart.

But if in your heart you would seek only love's peace and love's pleasure,

Then it is better for you that you cover your nakedness and pass out of love's threshing-floor,

Into the seasonless world where you shall laugh, but not all of your laughter, and weep, but not all of your tears.

Love gives naught but itself and takes naught but from itself.

Love possesses not nor would it be possessed;

For love is sufficient unto love.

When you love you should not say, "God is in my heart," but rather, "I am in the heart of God."

And think not you can direct the course of love, for love, if it finds you worthy, directs your course.

Love has no other desire but to fulfil itself.

But if you love and must needs have desires, let these be your desires:

To melt and be like a running brook that sings its melody to the night.

To know the pain of too much tenderness.

To be wounded by your own understanding of love;

And to bleed willingly and joyfully.

To wake at dawn with a winged heart and give thanks for another day of loving;

To rest at the noon hour and meditate love's ecstasy;

To return home at eventide with gratitude;

And then to sleep with a prayer for the beloved in your heart and a song of praise upon your lips.

The Prophet (Knopf, 1923).

ON JOY AND SORROW

Then a woman said, Speak to us of Joy and Sorrow.

And he answered:

Your joy is your sorrow unmasked.

And the selfsame well from which your laughter rises was oftentimes filled with your tears.

And how else can it be?

The deeper that sorrow carves into your being, the more joy you can contain.

Is not the cup that holds your wine the very cup that was burned in the potter's oven?

And is not the lute that soothes your spirit, the very wood that was hollowed with knives?

When you are joyous, look deep into your heart and you shall find it is only that which has given you sorrow that is giving you joy.

When you are sorrowful look again in your heart, and you shall see that in truth you are weeping for that which has been your delight.

Some of you say, "Joy is greater than sorrow," and others say, "Nay, sorrow is the greater."

But I say unto you, they are inseparable.

Together they come, and when one sits alone with you at
your board, remember that the other is asleep upon your bed.

Verily you are suspended like scales between your sorrow
and your joy.

Only when you are empty are you at standstill and balanced.

When the treasure-keeper lifts you to weigh his gold and his
silver, needs must your joy or your sorrow rise or fall.

(Published in Poem-a-Day on February 10, 2019, by the
Academy of American Poets- public domain)

ON GOOD AND EVIL

And one of the elders of the city said, Speak to us of Good and Evil.

And he answered:

Of the good in you I can speak, but not of the evil.

For what is evil but good tortured by its own hunger and thirst?

Verily when good is hungry it seeks food even in dark caves, and when it thirsts it drinks even of dead waters.

You are good when you are one with yourself.

Yet when you are not one with yourself you are not evil.

For a divided house is not a den of thieves; it is only a divided house.

And a ship without rudder may wander aimlessly among perilous isles yet sink not to the bottom.

You are good when you strive to give of yourself.

Yet you are not evil when you seek gain for yourself.

For when you strive for gain you are but a root that clings to the earth and sucks at her breast.

Surely the fruit cannot say to the root, "Be like me, ripe and full and ever giving of your abundance."

For to the fruit giving is a need, as receiving is a need to the root.

You are good when you are fully awake in your speech,

Yet you are not evil when you sleep while your tongue staggers without purpose.

And even stumbling speech may strengthen a weak tongue.

You are good when you walk to your goal firmly and with bold steps.

Yet you are not evil when you go thither limping.

Even those who limp go not backward.

But you who are strong and swift, see that you do not limp before the lame, deeming it kindness.

You are good in countless ways, and you are not evil when you are not good,

You are only loitering and sluggard.

Pity that the stags cannot teach swiftness to the turtles.

In your longing for your giant self lies your goodness: and that longing is in all of you.

But in some of you that longing is a torrent rushing with might to the sea, carrying the secrets of the hillsides and the songs of the forest.

And in others it is a flat stream that loses itself in angles and bends and lingers before it reaches the shore.

But let not him who longs much say to him who longs little, "Wherefore are you slow and halting?"

For the truly good ask not the naked, "Where is your garment?" nor the houseless, "What has befallen your house?"

The Prophet (Knopf, 1923).

ON FRIENDSHIP

And a youth said, Speak to us of Friendship.

And he answered, saying:

Your friend is your needs answered.

He is your field which you sow with love and reap with thanksgiving.

And he is your board and your fireside.

For you come to him with your hunger, and you seek him for peace.

When your friend speaks his mind, you fear not the "nay" in your own mind, nor do you withhold the "ay."

And when he is silent your heart ceases not to listen to his heart;

For without words, in friendship, all thoughts, all desires, all expectations are born and shared, with joy that is unacclaimed.

When you part from your friend, you grieve not;

For that which you love most in him may be clearer in his absence, as the mountain to the climber is clearer from the plain.

And let there be no purpose in friendship save the deepening of the spirit.

For love that seeks aught but the disclosure of its own mystery us not love but a net cast forth: and only the unprofitable is caught.

And let your best be for your friend.

If he must know the ebb of your tide, let him know its flood also.

For what is your friend that you should seek him with hours to kill?

Seek him always with hours to live.

For it is his to fill your need but not your emptiness.

And in the sweetness of friendship let there be laughter, and sharing of pleasures.

For in the dew of little things the heart finds its morning and is refreshed.

The Prophet (Knopf, 1923).

ON PAIN

And a woman spoke, saying, Tell us of Pain.

And he said:

Your pain is the breaking of the shell that encloses your understanding.

Even as the stone of the fruit must break, that its heart may stand in the sun, so must you know pain.

And could you keep your heart in wonder at the daily miracles of your life your pain would not seem less wondrous than your joy;

And you would accept the seasons of your heart, even as you have always accepted the seasons that pass over your fields.

And you would watch with serenity through the winters of your grief.

Much of your pain is self-chosen.

It is the bitter potion by which the physician within you heals your sick self.

Therefore, trust the physician, and drink his remedy in silence and tranquility:

For his hand, though heavy and hard, is guided by the tender hand of the Unseen,

And the cup he brings, though it burns your lips, has been fashioned of the clay which the Potter has moistened with His own sacred tears.

The Prophet (Knopf, 1923).

ON DEATH

Then Almitra spoke, saying, We would ask now of Death.

And he said:

You would know the secret of death.

But how shall you find it unless you seek it in the heart of
life?

The owl whose night-bound eyes are blind unto the day
cannot unveil the mystery of light.

If you would indeed behold the spirit of death, open your
heart wide unto the body of life.

For life and death are one, even as the river and the sea are
one.

In the depth of your hopes and desires lies your silent
knowledge of the beyond;

And like seeds dreaming beneath the snow your heart
dreams of spring.

Trust the dreams, for in them is hidden the gate to eternity.

Your fear of death is but the trembling of the shepherd when
he stands before the king whose hand is to be laid upon him
in honour.

Is the shepherd not joyful beneath his trembling, that he
shall wear the mark of the king?

47

Yet is he not more mindful of his trembling?

For what is it to die but to stand naked in the wind and to melt into the sun?

And what is it to cease breathing, but to free the breath from its restless tides, that it may rise and expand and seek God unencumbered?

Only when you drink from the river of silence shall you indeed sing.

And when you have reached the mountain top, then you shall begin to climb.

And when the earth shall claim your limbs, then shall you truly dance.

The Prophet (Knopf, 1923).

ON SELF-KNOWLEDGE

And a man said, Speak to us of Self-Knowledge.

And he answered, saying:

Your hearts know in silence the secrets of the days and the
nights.

But your ears thirst for the sound of your heart's knowledge.

You would know in words that which you have always
known in thought.

You would touch with your fingers the naked body of your
dreams.

And it is well you should.

The hidden well-spring of your soul must need rise and run
murmuring to the sea;

And the treasure of your infinite depths would be revealed to
your eyes.

But let there be no scales ot weigh your unknown treasure;

And seek not the depths of your knowledge with staff or
sounding line.

For self is a sea boundless and measureless.

Say not, "I have found the truth," but rather, "I have found a truth."

Say not, "I have found the path of the soul." Say rather, "I have met the soul walking upon my path."

For the soul walks upon all paths.

The soul walks not upon a line, neither does it grow like a reed.

The soul unfolds itself, like a lotus of countless petals.

The Prophet (Knopf, 1923)

ON TALKING

And then a scholar said, Speak of Talking.

And he answered, saying:

You talk when you cease to be at peace with your thoughts;

And when you can no longer dwell in the solitude of your heart you live in your lips, and sound is a diversion and a pastime.

And in much of your talking, thinking is half murdered.

For thought is a bird of space, that in a cage of words may indeed unfold its wings but cannot fly.

There are those among you who seek the talkative through fear of being alone.

The silence of aloneness reveals to their eyes their naked selves and they would escape.

And there are those who talk, and without knowledge or forethought reveal a truth which they themselves do not understand.

And there are those who have the truth within them, but they tell it not in words.

In the bosom of such as these the spirit dwells in rhythmic silence.

When you meet your friend on the roadside or in the market place, let the spirit in you move your lips and direct your tongue.

Let the voice within your voice speak to the ear or his ear;

For his soul will keep the truth of your heart as the taste of the wine is remembered

When the colour is forgotten and the vessel is no more.

The Prophet (Knopf, 1923)

ON TIME

And an astronomer said, Master, what of Time?

And he answered:

You would measure time the measureless and the immeasurable.

You would adjust your conduct and even direct the course of your spirit according to hours and seasons.

Of time you would make a stream upon whose bank you would sit and watch its flowing.

Yet the timeless in you is aware of life's timelessness,

And knows that yesterday is but today's memory and tomorrow is today's dream.

And that that which sings and contemplates in you is still dwelling within the bounds of that first moment which scattered the stars into space.

Who among you does not feel that his power to love is boundless?

And yet who does not feel that very love, though boundless, encompassed within the centre of his being, and moving not from love thought to love thought, nor from love deeds to other love deeds?

And is not time even as love is, undivided and spaceless?

But if in your thought you must measure time into seasons,
let each season encircle all the other seasons,

And let today embrace the past with remembrance and the
future with longing

The Prophet (Knopf, 1923)

ON GIVING

Then said a rich man, Speak to us of Giving.

And he answered:

You give but little when you give of your possessions.

It is when you give of yourself that you truly give.

For what are your possessions but things you keep and guard for fear you may need them tomorrow?

And tomorrow, what shall tomorrow bring to the overprudent dog burying bones in the trackless sand as he follows the pilgrims to the holy city?

And what is fear of need by need itself?

Is not dread of thirst when your well is full, the thirst that is unquenchable?

There are those who give little of the much which they have—and they give it for recognition and their hidden desire makes their gifts unwholesome.

And there are those who have little and give it all.

These are the believers in life and the bounty of life, and their coffer is never empty.

There are those who give with joy, and that joy is their reward.

And there are those who give with pain, and that pain is their baptism.

And there are those who give and know not pain in giving, nor do they seek joy, nor give with mindfulness of virtue;

They give as in yonder valley the myrtle breathes its fragrance into space.

Through the hands of such as these God speaks, and from behind their eyes. He smiles upon the earth.

It is well to give when asked, but it is better to give unasked, through understanding;

And to the open-handed the search for one who shall receive is joy greater than giving.

And is there aught you would withhold?

All you have shall some day be given;

Therefore give now, that the season of giving may be yours and not your inheritors'.

You often say, "I would give, but only to the deserving."

The trees in your orchard say not so, nor the flocks in your pasture.

They give that they may live, for to withhold is to perish.

Surely he who is worthy to receive his days and his nights, is worthy of all else from you.

And he who has deserved to drink from the ocean of life
deserves to fill his cup from your little stream.

And what desert greater shall there be, than that which lies in
the courage and the confidence, nay the charity, or receiving?

And who are you that men should rend their bosom and
unveil their pride, that you may see their worth naked and
their pride unabashed?

See first that you yourself deserve to be a giver, and an
instrument of giving.

For in truth it is life that gives unto life—while you, who
deem yourself a giver, are but a witness.

And you receivers—and you are all receivers—assume no
weight of gratitude, lest you lay a yoke upon yourself and
upon him who gives.

Rather rise together with the giver on his gifts as on wings;

For to be overmindful of your debt, is to doubt his generosity
who has the freehearted earth for mother, and God for father.

ON TEACHING

Then said a teacher, Speak to us of Teaching.

And he said:

No man can reveal to you aught but that which already lies half asleep in the dawning of your knowledge.

The teacher who walks in the shadow of the temple, among his followers, gives not of his wisdom but rather of his faith and his lovingness.

If he is indeed wise he does not bid you enter the house of his wisdom, but rather leads you to the threshold of your own mind.

The astronomer may speak to you of his understanding of space, but he cannot give you his understanding.

The musician may sing to you of the rhythm which is in all space, but he cannot give you the ear which arrests the rhythm nor the voice that echoes it.

And he who is versed in the science of numbers can tell of the regions of weight and measure, but he cannot conduct you thither.

For the vision of one man lends not its wings to another man.

And even as each one of you stands alone in God's knowledge, so must each one of you be alone in his knowledge of God and in his understanding of the earth.

The Prophet (Knopf, 1923)

ON MARRIAGE

Then Almitra spoke again and said, And what of Marriage, master?

And he answered saying:

You were born together, and together you shall be forevermore.

You shall be together when the white wings of death scatter your days.

Ay, you shall be together even in the silent memory of God.

But let there be spaces in your togetherness,

And let the winds of the heavens dance between you.

Love one another, but make not a bond of love:

Let it rather be a moving sea between the shores of your souls.

Fill each other's cup but drink not from one cup.

Give one another of your bread but eat not from the same loaf.

Sing and dance together and be joyous, but let each one of your be alone,

Even as the strings of the lute are alone though they quiver with the same music.

Give your hearts, but not into each other's keeping.

For only the hand of Life can contain your hearts.

And stand together yet not too near together:

For the pillars of the temple stand apart,

And the oak tree and the cypress grow not in each other's shadow.

The Prophet (Knopf, 1923)

ON BEAUTY

And a poet said, Speak to us of Beauty.

And he answered:

Where shall you seek beauty, and how shall your find her unless she herself be your way and your guide?

And how shall you speak of her except she be the weaver of your speech?

The aggrieved and the injured say, "Beauty is kind and gentle.

Like a young mother half-shy of her own glory she walks among us."

And the passionate say, "Nay, beauty is a thing of might and dread.

Like the tempest she shakes the earth beneath us and the sky above us."

The tired and the weary say, "Beauty is of soft whisperings. She speaks in our spirit.

Her voice yields to our silences like a faint light that quivers in fear of the shadow."

But the restless say, "We have heard her shouting among the mountains,

And with her cries came the sound of hoofs, and the beating
of wings and the roaring of lions."

At night the watchmen of the city say, "Beauty shall rise with
the dawn from the east."

And at noontide the toilers and the wayfarers say, "We have
seen her leaning over the earth from the windows of the
sunset."

In winter say the snow-bound, "She shall come with the
spring leaping upon the hills."

And in the summer heat the reapers say, "We have seen her
dancing with the autumn leaves, and we saw a drift of snow
in her hair."

All these things have you said of beauty,

Yet in truth you spoke not of her but of needs unsatisfied,

And beauty is not a need but an ecstasy

It is not a mouth thirsting nor an empty hand stretched forth,

But rather a heart enflamed and a soul enchanted.

It is not in the image you would see nor the song you would
hear,

But rather an image you see though you close your eyes and a
song you hear though you shut your ears.

It is not the sap within the furrowed bark, nor a wing attached to a claw,

But rather a garden for ever in bloom and a flock of angels for ever in flight.

People of Orphalese, beauty is life when life unveils her holy face.

But you are life and you are the veil.

Beauty is eternity gazing at itself in a mirror.

But you are eternity and you are the mirror.

The Prophet (Knopf, 1923)

ON WORK

Then a ploughman said, Speak to us of Work.

And he answered, saying:

You work that you may keep pace with the earth and the soul of the earth.

For to be idle is to become a stranger unto the seasons, and to step out of life's procession, that marches in majesty and proud submission towards the infinite.

When you work you are a flute through whose heart the whispering of the hours turns to music.

Which of you would be a reed, dumb and silent, when all else sings together in unison?

Always you have been told that work is a curse and labour a misfortune.

But I say to you that when you work you fulfil a part of earth's furthest dream, assigned to you when the dream was born,

And in keeping yourself with labour you are in truth loving life,

And to love life through labour is to be intimate with life's inmost secret.

But if you in your pain call birth an affliction and the support of the flesh a curse written upon your brow, then I answer that naught but the sweat of your brow shall wash away that which is written.

You have been told also that life is darkness, and in your weariness you echo what was said by the weary.

And I say that life is indeed darkness save when there is urge,

And all urge is blind save when there is knowledge,

And all knowledge is vain save when there is work,

And all work is empty save when there is love;

And when you work with love you bind yourself to yourself, and to one another, and to God.

And what is it to work with love?

It is to weave the cloth with threads drawn from your heart, even as if your beloved were to wear that cloth.

It is to build a house with affection, even as if your beloved were to dwell in that house.

It is to sow seeds with tenderness and reap the harvest with joy, even as if your beloved were to eat the fruit.

It is to charge all things you fashion with a breath of your own spirit,

And to know that all the blessed dead are standing about you and watching.

Often have I heard you say, as if speaking in sleep, "He who works in marble, and finds the shape of his own soul in the stone, is nobler than he who ploughs the soil.

And he who seizes the rainbow to lay it on a cloth in the likeness of man, is more than he who makes the sandals for our feet."

But I say, not in sleep but in the overwakefulness of noontide, that the wind speaks not more sweetly to the giant oaks than to the least of all the blades of grass;

And he alone is great who turns the voice of the wind into a song made sweeter by his own loving.

Work is love made visible.

And if you cannot work with love but only with distaste, it is better that you should leave your work and sit at the gate of the temple and take alms of those who work with joy.

For if you bake bread with indifference, you bake a bitter bread that feeds but half man's hunger.

And if you grudge the crushing of the grapes, your grudge distils a poison in the wine.

And if you sing though as angels, and love not the singing, you muffle man's ears to the voices of the day and the voices of the night.

The Prophet (Knopf, 1923)

ON EATING AND DRINKING

Then an old man, a keeper of an inn, said, Speak to us of Eating and Drinking.

And he said:

Would that you could live on the fragrance of the earth, and like an air plant be sustained by the light.

But since you must kill to eat, and rob the newly born of its mother's milk to quench your thirst, let it then be an act of worship.

And let your board stand an altar on which the pure and the innocent of forest and plain are sacrificed for that which is purer and still more innocent in man.

When you kill a beast say to him in your heart,

"By the same power that slays you, I too am slain; and I too shall be consumed.

For the law that delivered you into my hand shall deliver me into a mightier hand.

Your blood and my blood is naught but the sap that feeds the tree of heaven."

And when you crush an apple with your teeth, say to it in your heart,

"Your seeds shall live in my body,

And the buds of your tomorrow shall blossom in my heart,

And your fragrance shall be my breath,

And together we shall rejoice through all the seasons."

And in the autumn, when you gather the grapes of your vineyards for the winepress, say in your heart,

"I too am a vineyard, and my fruit shall be gathered for the winepress,

And like new wine I shall be kept in eternal vessels."

And in winter, when you draw the wine, let there be in your heart a song for each cup;

And let there be in the song a remembrance for the autumn days, and for the vineyard, and for the winepress.

The Prophet (Knopf, 1923)

ON RELIGION

And an old priest said, Speak to us of Religion.

And he said:

Have I spoken this day of aught else?

Is not religion all deeds and all reflection,

And that which is neither deed nor reflection, but a wonder
and a surprise ever springing in the soul, even while the
hand hew the stone or tend the loom?

Who can separate his faith from his actions, or his belief from
his occupations?

Who can spread his hours before him, saying, "This for God
and this for myself' This for my soul, and this other for my
body?"

All your hours are wings that beat through space from self to
self.

He who wears his morality but as his best garment were
better naked.

The wind and the sun will tear no holes in his skin.

And he who defines his conduct by ethics imprisons his
song-bird in a cage.

The freest song comes not through bars and wires.

And he to whom worshipping is a window, to open but also to shut, has not yet visited the house of his soul whose windows are from dawn to dawn.

Your daily life is your temple and your religion.

Whenever you enter into it take with you your all.

Take the plough and the forge and the mallet and the lute,

The things you have fashioned in necessity or for delight.

For in revery you cannot rise above your achievements nor fall lower than your failures.

And take with you all men:

For in adoration you cannot fly higher than their hopes nor humble yourself lower than their despair.

And if you would know God be not therefore a solver of riddles.

Rather look about you and you shall see Him playing with your children.

And look into space; you shall see Him walking in the cloud, outstretching His arms in the lightning and descending in rain.

You shall see Him smiling in flowers, then rising and waving His hands in trees.

ON FREEDOM

And an orator said, Speak to us of Freedom.

And he answered:

At the city gate and by your fireside I have seen you prostrate yourself and worship your own freedom,

Even as slaves humble themselves before a tyrant and praise him though he slays them.

Ay, in the grove of the temple and in the shadow of the citadel I have seen the freest among you wear their freedom as a yoke and a handcuff.

And my heart bled within me; for you can only be free when even the desire of seeking freedom becomes a harness to you, and when you cease to speak of freedom as a goal and a fulfilment.

You shall be free indeed when your days are not without a care nor your nights without a want and a grief,

But rather when these things girdle your life and yet your rise above them naked and unbound.

And how shall you rise beyond your days and nights unless you break the chains which you at the dawn of your understanding have fastened around your noon hour?

In truth that which you call freedom is the strongest of these chains, though its links glitter in the sun and dazzle your eyes.

And what is it but fragments of your own self you would discard that you may become free?

If it is an unjust law you would abolish, that law was written with your own hand upon your own forehead.

You cannot erase it by burning your law books nor by washing the foreheads of your judges, though you pour the sea upon them.

And if it is a despot you would dethrone, see first that his throne erected within you is destroyed.

For how can a tyrant rule the free and the proud, but for a tyranny in their own freedom and a shame in their own pride?

And if it is a care you would cast off, that care has been chosen by you rather than imposed upon you.

And if it is a fear you would dispel, the seat of that fear is in your heart and not in the hand of the feared.

Verily all things move within your being in constant half embrace, the desired and the dreaded, the repugnant and the cherished, the pursued and that which you would escape.

These things move within you as lights and shadows in pairs that cling.

And when the shadow fades and is no more, the light that lingers becomes a shadow to another light.

And thus your freedom when it loses its fetters becomes itself the fetter of a greater freedom.

The Prophet (Knopf, 1923)

MORE BOOKS BY THE AUTHOR

RUMI-DROPS of ENLIGHTENMENT: (Quotes & Poems)

Available on Amazon:

https://www.amazon.com/dp/B09VCLHV2V

Kindle: **(ASIN: B09VCLHV2V)**
Paperback: (**ISBN-13: 979-8430816995)**

THE AI THOUGHT BOOK

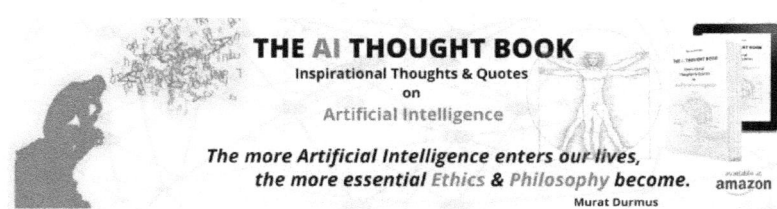

Available on Amazon:

https://www.amazon.com/dp/B08Z4BWN1X

Kindle: **(ASIN: B08Z4BWN1X)**
Paperback: **(ISBN-13: 979-8718051674)**

An excerpt of the book can be downloaded here:

THOUGHT-PROVOKING QUOTES & CONTEMPLATIONS FROM FAMOUS PSYCHOLOGISTS

(Over 600 Quotes & Contemplations)

Available on Amazon:

Kindle: **(ASIN: B09B79KR7P)**
Paperback: **(ISBN-13: 979-8543952337)**

THOUGHT-PROVOKING QUOTES & CONTEMPLATIONS FROM FAMOUS PHYSICISTS

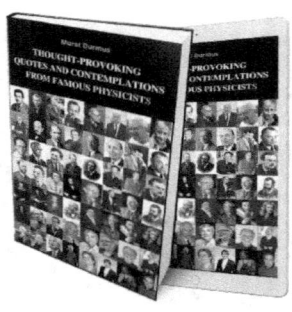

Quotes and Contemplations from famous Physicists that will change your view of Life and the Nature of Things.

"Somewhere, something incredible is waiting to be known."

~ Carl Sagan

Available on Amazon:

Kindle:	**(ASIN: B09B79KR7P)**
Paperback:	**(ISBN-13: 979-8543952337)**
Hardcover:	**(ISBN-13: 979-8545176274)**

INSIDE ALAN TURING: QUOTES & CONTEMPLATIONS

Alan Turing is generally considered the father of computer science and artificial intelligence. He was also a theoretical biologist who developed algorithms to explain complex patterns using simple inputs and random fluctuation as a side hobby. Unfortunately, his life tragically ended in suicide in 1954, after he was chemically castrated as punishment (instead of prison) for 'criminal' gay acts.

"We can only see a short distance ahead, but we can see plenty there that needs to be done." ~ Alan Turing

Available on Amazon:

Kindle: **(ASIN: B09K3669BX)**
Paperback: **(ISBN- 979-8751495848)**